For Deniz

© Copyright 2014

Written by Sally A Jones and Amanda C Jones
Illustrations by Annalisa C Jones

Published by GUINEA PIG EDUCATION

2 Cobs Way,
New Haw,
Addlestone,
Surrey,
KT15 3AF.
www.guineapigeducation.co.uk

NO part of this publication may be reproduced, stored or copied for commercial purposes and profit without the prior written permission of the publishers.

ISBN: 978-1-907733-82-6

Dear Kids and Parents,

This book contains a structured course to teach children to spell using phonics.

A friendly character, an alien called Zoggy, takes your child on a journey: first, he introduces single consonant and vowel sounds; secondly, he teaches them to blend sounds together to form consonant blends; and then, he introduces a series of middle sounds.

Each challenge includes funny phonic rhymes, phrases and sentences to reinforce the sounds being taught; learn them off by heart, practise rewriting them from memory. There are also a series of exercises to help your child practise spelling, including tests where your child can read, copy, cover and spell.

MEET Zoggy...

ZOGGY has been sent from planet ZEN, three million light years away.

MY MISSION: to help you guys on earth to improve your spelling.

WHY ME? Zoggies have computer brains when it comes to spelling, as we have a built in spellcheck.

Work through the challenges and I will teach you to spell using phonics, as I explore Earth.

REPORT BACK TO PLANET ZEN...

HAVE JUST LANDED MY SPACE CRAFT ON EARTH...
EXPLORING!

ZOGGY'S FIRST CHALLENGE

Zoggy says, "Do you know the letters of the alphabet?"

A	B	C	D
E	F	G	H
I	J	K	L
M	N	O	P
Q	R	S	T
U	V	W	X
Y	Z		

ZOGGY'S SECOND CHALLENGE

Zoggy says,

"Use the letters of the alphabet to sound out the words below."

The middle sounds are **vowels** - a,e,o,i,u.

All the other sounds are called **consonants**.

```
d o g    f o x    h e n    g o t    j o t    k i t

l o t    n o t    m e n    p e n    qu i t   r a t

s a t    t e n    v e t    f i t    y e t    Z e n
```

Use these to sound out longer words, like:

fan tas tic   or   a li en

ZOGGY'S THIRD CHALLENGE

Zoggy makes three letter words.

REPORT BACK TO PLANET ZEN...

I have seen a fat pig on planet earth

    Pig sits by the bin
    and sips from a tin.

    He digs in the mud
    to get a fat bug.

ZOGGY'S FOURTH CHALLENGE

Zoggy makes a list of places he wants to visit on earth. He uses words with single syllable sounds.

AMERICA	ITALY	JAPAN
POLAND	LAPLAND	CANADA
ROMANIA	MEXICO	EGYPT
TEXAS	INDIA	FLORIDA

Zoggy says:

"Find more words with these sounds."

SH	CH
SHIP	CHIN

WH	TH
WHAT	THIN

Find words for each sound. Use a reading book to help you.

Time for a test.

READ	COPY	COVER & SPELL
path		
bath		
shop		
dash		
rash		
chin		
chop		
much		
such		
lunch		
wash		
wish		
fish		
rich		

Tricky words to remember.

READ	COPY	COVER & SPELL
there		
then		
they		
their		
those		
were		
when		
where		

ZOGGY'S FIFTH CHALLENGE

Zoggy says:

"Now, blend sounds together to make new words."

D + R = DR as in **<u>DRUM</u>**

Fill in his report.

c	r	cr	crab	a creature found in the sea
g	r	.....	....	....
p	r	.....	....	....
t	r	.....	....	....
f	r	.....	....	....
b	r	.....	....	....
s	l	.....	....	....
g	l	.....	....	....
f	l	.....	....	....
b	l	.....	....	....
c	l	.....	....	....
p	l	.....	....	....
s	n	.....	....	....
t	r	.....	....	....
s	k	.....	....	....
s	p	.....	....	....
s	c	.....	....	....

He uses double consonant blends.

Read the funny phonic sentences.

REPORT BACK TO PLANET ZEN...

OBSERVATIONS OF EARTH:

BABY

Baby **grins**,
Sits in his **pram**,
Claps his hands,
Bangs on his **drum**,
Holds his soft felt dog.
Clenches his pink fist
And **drinks** some milk.

CAT

Soft cat
Holds his felt frog,
Sings a song to himself,
(Purr) (Purr)
Drinks milk from his dish.

HEDGEHOG

Hog rests,
Sips milk,
Digs in the sand and
Pads on the soft mud.

SLUG

Slimy slug
Slips
And slithers
Along the flat path.

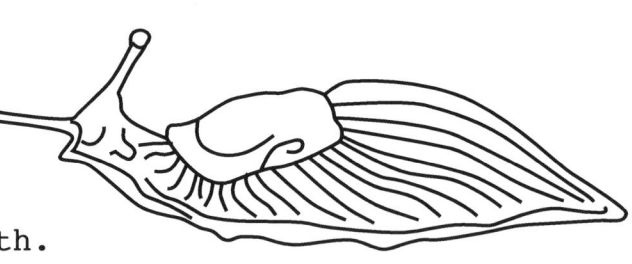

FROG

Frog flips,
Flops on his belly
And jumps up the grassy
bank.

Time for a test.

READ	COPY	COVER & SPELL
grins		
pram		
claps		
drum		
clench		
drink		
crash		
plot		
grass		
spot		
flop		
hands		
bangs		
soft		
felt		
pink		
fist		
milk		
rests		
hold		
himself		
sing song		

ZOGGY'S SIXTH CHALLENGE

"I need to find double consonant blends to help me write about earth. Can you help me?"

Help Zoggy find words for each sound.

ck	ct	mp	nd	ng	nk	nt
sick	act	camp	handle	bring	think	went

... lt	... lk	... st	... ft	... lp	... ss	... lf
felt	milk	rest	soft	help	kiss	himself

"I also need to find triple consonant blends to help me."

scr	shr	sph	spl	spr	squ	str
scratch	shred	sphere	splash	sprint	squash	strap

... thr	... tch	... dge
throb	ditch	edge

MESSAGE TO PLANET ZEN..

OBSERVATIONS OF EARTH:

    KIDS HELP!!!

<u>KIDS:</u>

Get sick
Play tricks

Love to act
Learn some facts

Go to camp
Sit under a lamp

Do hand stands
Put on top brands

Sing a song
Take too long

Go to Kent
Sleep in a tent

Make things in felt
Wear a thick belt

Drink milk
Wear silk

Like to rest
Try their best

Kiss the dog
Miss the jog.

HUMAN - GIRL

Fall in a stinging nettle patch,
Get a scratch.

Use Dads shredder,
Get redder and redder.

Splash in a puddle,
Get in a muddle.

Spray the room,
So it smells like a bloom.

Run up the street,
Sit on the seat.

Throw a ball,
See it fall.

Stand on the edge,
Hide under the hedge.

Play squash,
Forget to wash.

But, most of all...

Kids love to go
splashing in
squishy,
squashy,
squelchy mud.

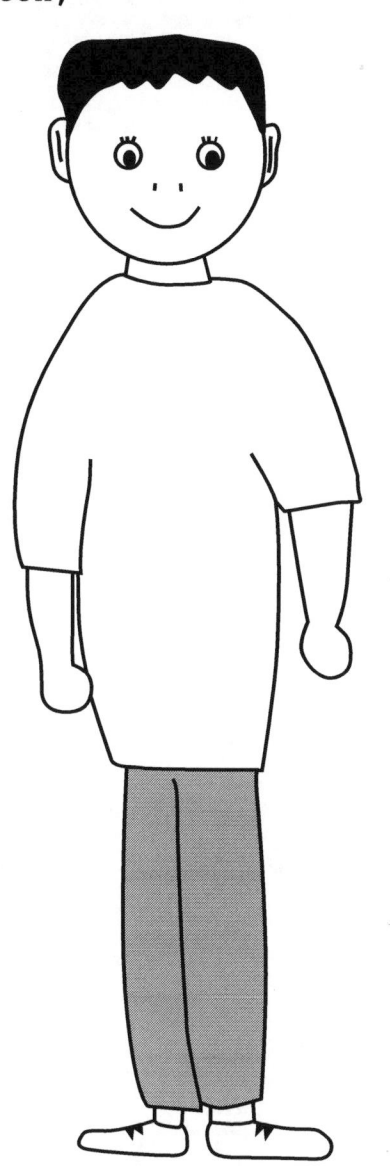

HUMAN - BOY

Time for a test.

READ	COPY	COVER & SPELL
think		
sink		
sank		
link		
mink		
pink		
rink		
tinker		
sprinkle		
crinkle		
thank		
bank		
rank		
tank		
stand		
stick		
trick		
act		
fact		
camp		
lamp		
handstand		
brand		
song		

Time for a test.

READ	COPY	COVER & SPELL
long		
tent		
scratch		
latch		
catch		
match		
batch		
hatch		
latch		
patch		
witch		
hitch		
pitch		
stitch		
stinging		
shred		
splash		
string		
thing		
edge		
hedge		
squash		
splashing		
squelchy		

ZOGGY'S SEVENTH CHALLENGE

Let's learn another sound.

ZOOM...

TO PLANET EARTH IN A
ROCKET

To learn that <u>C</u> and <u>K</u> make <u>ck</u>.

PREPARE FOR TAKE OFF!

5
4
3
2
1

THE ROCKET
BLASTS
OFF...

```
Learn to read sounds
with two syllables.
```

Break down the word
rock et
into two syllables.

Run the sounds
bl ast
together

Zoggy says:

"I travel across earth in a jet and take stock of the planet, to teach you the sound ck."

MESSAGE TO PLANET ZEN...

AIR FLIGHT:

- <u>Pack</u> bags
- <u>Stack</u> them in the taxi
- <u>Lock</u> the door
- <u>Check</u> in at the airport
- <u>Pick</u> up boarding passes
- Put hand luggage on the <u>rack</u>
- Take off and watch the <u>clock tick</u> on

From the air I see:

Flats in **blocks**.

Beaches full of **rocks**.

Ships in their **docks.**

Birds in **flocks**.

Ticking **clocks**.

Shops full of... **socks!**

Zoggy says,

"Back on land, I can teach you sounds with two syllables."

rabbit	robin
kitten	lion
camel	squirrel
zebra	puppy
dragon	falcon
chicken	lizard
wombat	panda

Can you think of any other animals that can be broken down with two or three syllables, like: kang a roo?

MESSAGE TO PLANET ZEN...

The people of earth pack picnics in baskets, with flasks of lemon and plastic cups. Then, they sit on a blanket on the grass.

Typical humans talk like this:

"Kim, see that rabbit near the plant?" says Mum.
"Sam, mind that wasp doesn't sting you," adds Dad.
"Mum, can I go on the swing?"
"Can I have some more crisps?" demand the kids.

Time for a test.

READ	COPY	COVER & SPELL
thick		
thicken		
lick		
flick		
stick		
tickle		
tackle		
struck		
truck		
trick		
trickle		
track		
brick		
bracken		
rocket		
interesting		
stamp		
crust		
clinic		
hospital		
picnic		
comical		
flask of lemon		
plastic		
blanket		
rabbit		
string		
chicken		
kangaroo		

ZOGGY'S EIGHTH CHALLENGE

Be cool and learn
'oo' and 'oo'.

Zoggy says,

"What can I do to teach you 'oo' sounds?"

Be **cool** in a **pool**.

Wear a **hood** in the **wood**.

Put some **blooms** in a **cool room**.

Fly a **balloon** up to the **moon**.

Play **snooker**.

Ride a **scooter**.

Go out in the **gloom**. See a spooky witch on a **broom**.

See a rook **swoop**, an owl **hoot** and a burglar with his **loot**.

Is it **too soon** to have lunch at **noon**?

MESSAGE TO PLANET ZEN...

GOT SOME GOOD FOOD. YUM!!!

I stood on a stool to get a cookery book from the shelf and fell off. I was choosing some good food to cook on my cooker for a snack in the afternoon.

Read the 'oo' words.

looked	looking	took	hook	rook
cook	cooker	cooking	shook	brook
crook	good	foot	soot	sooty
hood	moor	poor	poorly	goodness
misunderstood	understood	stood	stool	spool
school	fool	foolish	forsook	mistook
moon	soon	loom	zoo	room
moo	snooker	gloom	groom	broom
swoop	scoop	scoot	scooter	spoon
hoot	hooting	shoot	choose	choosing
too	boot	boots	scoop	balloon
harpoon	maroon	spook	food	mood

How many can you remember?

Compete the list:

oo	oo
cool	book
fool	look
soon	hood
moon	

Time for a test.

READ	COPY	COVER & SPELL
moon		
soon		
zoo		
room		
moo		
snooker		
groom		
broom		
swoop		
scoop		
harpoon		
maroon		
mood		
scooter		
spoon		
hoot		
hooting		
scoop		
choosing		
too		
boot		
boots		
balloon		
spook		
food		

READ	COPY	COVER & SPELL
look		
looking		
hook		
rook		
cook		
cooker		
cooking		
poor		
poorly		
stood		
misunderstood		
book		
crook		
good		
food		
soot		
sooty		
hood		
moor		
school		
fool		
foolish		
mistook		

ZOGGY'S NINTH CHALLENGE

Zoggy says:

How do you feel about learning a new sound 'ee' and 'ea'?

Zoggy says, "What can I do to teach you the sound 'ee' and 'ea'?"

Speed in a **jeep**.

Creep up a **street**.

Sleep for a **week**.

Feed on **meat**.

Eat peaches

and **cream**

for a **treat**.

Freezing!

Read, cover and write.

> **MESSAGE TO PLANET ZEN...**
>
> I am sleeping by the stream and dreaming real
> dreams. Green leaves rustle in the breeze. A
> moorhen swims in the reeds, a robin cheeps, bees
> suck sweet nectar and sheep with thick fleece feed.
> It is so ideal. It doesn't feel real.

Read these 'ee' words.

tree	see	bee	knee	queen
sees	seen	free	sweep	keep
sheep	cheep	cheese	peep	weep
creep	steep	street	speed	speeding
succeed	seek	leek	meek	cheek
breed	creed	screech	heed	need
weed	feed	free	exceed	sleep
fleece	feel	sweet	feet	seed
wheel	squeeze			

Read these 'ea' words.

speak	dream	stream	cream	breach
lead	steal	scream	beach	teach
teacher	creature	preach	preacher	flea
plea	please	treason	heal	sea
crease	lease	grease	real	meal
beat	seat	wheat	heat	eat
meat	neat	peat	pleat	treat
reap	reach	breathe	recreation	crease
ceased				

How many can you remember?

Time for a test.

READ	COPY	COVER & SPELL
seen		
took		
tree		
cooking		
bedrooms		
school		
teeth		
shook		
speed		
understood		
hoot		
stream		
shoot		
dream		
scooter		
creature		
spoon		
please		
balloon		
teacher		

ZOGGY'S TENTH CHALLENGE

Go out in the car to learn the sound 'ar'.

Zoggy says, "What can I do to teach you the sound 'ar'?"

"Charming!"

Start the car; travel far.

See Farmer Mark in the barn on the farm.

See a horse that pulls a cart.

See a harvester cutting the corn.

See a farmer's market selling marmalade tart.

See a large dog bark, bark, bark!

MESSAGE TO PLANET ZEN...

FIREWORKS PARTY STARTS AT 8PM.

ZOGGY IS THE STAR PART!!!

Stars sparkling
In the dark,
Remarkable!

Zoggy is alarmed,
there is risk of being harmed.

Read these 'ar' words.

are	car	bar	far	jar
char	arm	charm	charming	alarm
park	dark	lark	bark	hark
mark	parked	spark	shark	large
larger	largest	part	cart	tart
start	card	hard	particular	parted
party	March	starch	march	artist
barn	farmer	harvest	harvester	depart
departure	compartment	department	sharp	parliament

How many can you remember?

Time for a test.

READ	COPY	COVER & SPELL
are		
car		
bar		
far		
jar		
char		
arm		
charming		
alarm		
park		
dark		
lark		
bark		
hark		
mark		
parked		
spark		
shark		
large		
larger		

READ	COPY	COVER & SPELL
largest		
part		
card		
tart		
start		
yard		
harvester		
hard		
particular		
parted		
party		
March		
starch		
artist		
barn		
farmer		
harvest		
depart		
departure		
compartment		
department		

CHALLENGE ELEVEN

Go to the store at four
to learn the sound 'or'.

Zoggy says,

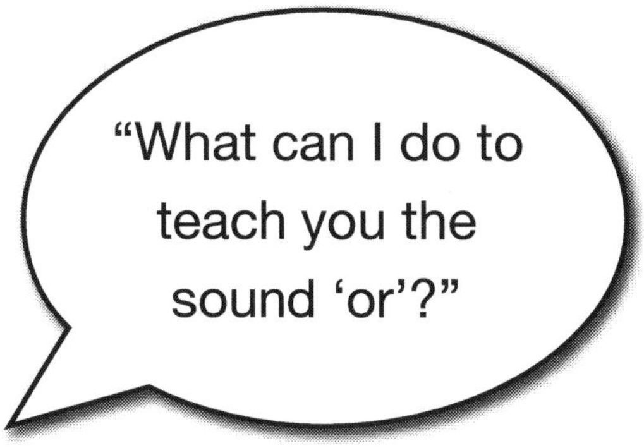

"What can I do to teach you the sound 'or'?"

Go to the **store** at four.

Eat like a **horse**;

Food of every **sort**.

Buy sweets **galore**.

Try apples with no **core**.

Spill **corn** flakes all over the floor.

Eat **more** and **more**!

" I need to do some sports after all this food. Maybe I could swim along the shore...'

MESSAGE TO PLANET ZEN...

Online Book Store

I have ordered an enormous pile of storybooks from an online store, so I can read them as I orbit the earth. They will inform me about life on earth.

Read these 'or' words.

for	bore	core	sore	more
tore	shore	chore	ignore	store
score	horse	enormous	ford	cord
lord	border	bordering	inform	form
sort	port	short	sport	corn
corner	corners	order	orders	galore
born	story	Lorna	storm	horse

How many can you remember?

Time for a test.

READ	COPY	COVER & SPELL
for		
bore		
core		
sore		
more		
tore		
shore		
chore		
ignore		
store		
score		
horse		
enormous		
ford		
cord		
storm		
lord		
border		
bordering		
inform		

READ	COPY	COVER & SPELL
form		
sort		
port		
short		
sport		
corn		
corner		
order		
galore		
born		
story		
Lorna		

ZOGGY'S TWELFTH CHALLENGE

Zoggy goes to a masked ball.

Three tricky sounds to explore: 'er' 'ur' 'ir'

Zoggy says,

"Where can I go to teach you the sounds 'ur', 'ir' and 'er'?"

Match the place to its event.

More Marvellous Monster Discoveries stored here at the...	**Church Hall**
Birthday parties for mothers, fathers, brothers and sisters at the...	**Art Gallery**
Major works of art by modern artists at the ...	**Festival Hall**
Grand Bazaar starts at two o'clock. To be opened by the Curly Whirly Monster.	**Ranjit's Cafe**
The mayor invites you to the third monster mask ball at... on the thirteenth of November at seven o'clock. You will have an evening of first class entertainment. Dinner with cabaret, including surprise appearance by... Come and have a wonderful time!	**Curly Whirly Monster Museum**

MESSAGE TO PLANET ZEN...

I am in the monster gallery at the museum, staring up at a model of an enormous creature called the Curly Whirly Monster. A tractor driver discovered the monster, that lived on earth millions of years ago, on a farm. An expert confirmed that it was an important discovery and offered him a reward.

"I need to start digging."

"I might find more treasure discoveries from the third century..."

Revise these tricky sounds.

Read Zoggy's message to planet Zen. Find out what he had observed and learn to spell at the same time. Write each sound word in the right column.

AR	OR

UR	IR

ER

Read and write these 'ur' and 'ir' words.

fur	purr	turn	burn	curl
burst	shirt	stir	fir	first
firm	birthday	curler	unfurl	turning
burning	turned	third	skirt	girls
dirty	churn	burned	return	returning
returnable	thirty	firm	bird	curl
turn	surprise	treasure	urgently	urchin
absurd	Thursday	thirsty	nurse	murmur

Time for a test.

READ	COPY	COVER & SPELL
burst		
purple		
turning		
returnable		
surprise		
treasure		
thirsty		
Thursday		
first		
dirty		
stirring		
skirt		
third		
circus		
birthday		
murmur		
thirty		
urchin		
burning		

Read and write these 'er' words.

fern	her	mother	father	sister
brother	bigger	smaller	larger	taller
shorter	farmer	reporter	builder	photographer
paper	newspaper	water	weather	thunder
whether	shelter	layer	never	clever
Heather	feather	leather	together	shoulder
finger	harder	lower	higher	closer
answer	larder	supper	dinner	river
camera	wonder	interest	interested	under
underneath	discovery	discover	discovered	wonder
wonderful	clerk	other	offer	corner
prefer	consider	considerable	border	disorder
after	afternoon	observe	observer	observation
shiver	splinter	winner	bewilder	bewilderment
different	interrupt	exasperated	another	perform
performance	anniversary	summer	remember	remembered
winter	determine			

Time for a test.

READ	COPY	COVER & SPELL
finger		
perform		
afternoon		
closer		
dinner		
river		
summer		
wonderful		
discovered		
underneath		
weather		
photographer		
together		
interrupted		
determine		
remember		
different		
interested		
perfect		
observe		

Time for a test.

CHALLENGE THIRTEEN

I want to go away on holiday in May, to Sandy Bay, lay on the beach all day and feel the spray to learn 'ay' sounds.

Zoggy says,

"What can I do to teach you 'ai' or 'ay' sounds?"

Catch a **train.**
Play in the **rain.**

Organise a **display.**
Go on **holiday.**

Take a yacht for a **sail.**
Go to the woods for a nature **trail.**

Eat lunch by a **bay.**
Make pots with **clay.**

See my football team **play,**
At home or **away**.

MESSAGE TO PLANET ZEN...

Fishing with some bait, I put my line down and wait and wait. Why am I still waiting for a catch?

Read and write these 'ai' and 'ay' words.

rain	grain	railway	train	straight
sail	chain	bait	waiting	daisy
remain	restrain	pain	main	brain
straight	explain	plain	stain	stairs

day	bay	May	play	stay
away	hay	crayon	Monday	stray
ray	tray	fray	pray	lay
birthday	always	daydream	holiday	yesterday

Time for a test.

READ	COPY	COVER & SPELL
rain		
main		
raining		
rail		
trail		
grain		
brain		
pain		
again		
strain		
drain		
straight		
wait		
waiting		
explain		
remain		
restrain		
noise		

READ	COPY	COVER & SPELL
day		
say		
May		
play		
crayon		
ray		
stray		
stay		
pray		
yesterday		
tray		
fray		
playing		
way		
Monday		
always		
daydream		
holiday		

CHALLENGE FOURTEEN

What is that noise?
It is annoying me but
it teaches you 'oi'
and 'oy' sounds.

Zoggy says,

"What can I do to teach you 'oi' or 'oy' sounds?"

Play with some **toys,**
Meant for **boys.**

Spoil my notebook
With untidy writing.

Make some good **choices:**
Join a club, a **choir**, an orchestra.

Boil some fish and **oysters**
To make an **enjoyable** soup.

Scream at the top of my **voice.**
Point someone in the right direction.

Be **annoyed**
Because it always rains.

Be **disappointed;**
I missed seeing the **Royal** Queen of England.

Rejoice! I am here on earth.

MESSAGE TO PLANET ZEN...

Troy the boy next door is too noisy. He makes too much noise with his rock music. I am boiling over. The noise is spoiling my day. I cannot avoid it, even if I go into the toilet. It is like poison to my ears. I am very disappointed. What tactics should I employ to stop his annoying noise?

Read and write these 'oi' and 'oy' words.

boil	boiled	boiling	toil	soil
foil	noise	noisy	join	joining
choice	rejoice	avoid	coin	moisture
voice	toilet	toiletry		

boy	toy	joy	Roy	royal
enjoy	envoy	enjoyed	destroy	employ
oyster	annoy	loyal	cowboy	decoy

Time for a test.

READ	COPY	COVER & SPELL
boil		
boiled		
toil		
spoil		
foil		
noise		
noisy		
join		
joining		
choice		
rejoice		
avoid		
coin		
moisture		
voice		
toilet		
adjoin		
point		

READ	COPY	COVER & SPELL
boy		
toy		
joy		
royal		
Roy		
enjoy		
envoy		
enjoyed		
enjoyable		
employ		
employable		
annoy		
loyal		
cowboy		
decoy		
disappointed		
disappointing		
destroy		

CHALLENGE FIFTEEN

Zoggy prowls round the wild wood at dusk to teach you 'ou' and 'ow' sounds.

Zoggy says,

"What can I do to teach you 'ow' or 'ou' sounds?"

Go **down**

To the dense, dark wood,

A squirrel runs in the leafy **boughs**.

Observe a **brown owl** hoot,

A lone wolf **howl**,

A hungry predator **prowl**,

A snarling wildcat **pounce**,

And the timid **mouse bounce**

Round in the hedge.

Be brave...

The wild wood is not for **cowards**.

Zoggy looks down from the south tower. Thick cloud... Oh no! Surely not another shower of rain again.

It is a long way to the ground, but he is not a coward. Even on a cloudy day, Zoggy can see all around the town. He sees thousands of houses with flowers in their gardens.

MESSAGE TO PLANET ZEN...

Stray dog walking down the town street

I met a huge hairy hound with a wide open mouth. I am not a coward, but I let out a loud sound, because I had not encountered a creature like this before. He bounded up to me with a grin and licked my outstretched metal hand. Have I found a new friend?

Time for a test.

READ	COPY	COVER & SPELL
crowd		
town		
towel		
owl		
coward		
shower		
tower		
allow		
allowance		
crowned		
cloud		
mouth		
hound		
around		
wound		
trousers		
ground		
shout		
outstretched		
encountered		

CHALLENGE SIXTEEN

Zoggy says,

"A <u>famous</u> cousin from the country teaches you silent 'ou' sounds."

Zoggy says,

"What can I do to teach you silent 'ou'?"

The **famous** cousin lives in the country.

He has a **fabulous** horse.

He is an outstanding rider, who competes in lots of show jumping events.

His trophies **encourage** him to win.

His mum cooks **nourishing** recipes like cookie **dough**.

Fabulous! **Marvellous! Incredulous! Courageous**!

Living **dangerously**!

CHALLENGE SEVENTEEN

Row, row the boat, along the slow flowing river, as the sun slowly sinks lower and lower into the horizon, teaches you 'oa' and 'ow' sounds.

Zoggy says,

"When two vowels go a walking, the first one does the talking to learn the sound 'oa'?"

"What can I do to teach you 'oa' or 'ow' sounds?

Moan

Groan

Wash with **soap**

Float my **boat**

Get a sore **throat**

Eat hot **toast**

Drive to the **coast**

Act like a **goat**

Score a **goal**.

MESSAGE TO PLANET ZEN...

What I see on a winter's day...

The wind
Blows hard
Making the
Old branches
Of the the oak
Tree groan.

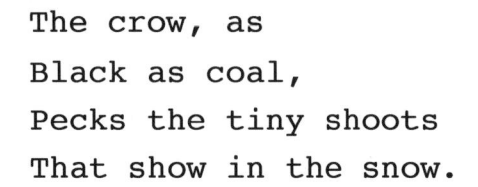

The crow, as
Black as coal,
Pecks the tiny shoots
That show in the snow.

An old fellow follows
The snowy road,
In a ragged
Soaking wet coat.

He approaches the village;
He sees the glowing light
From the church window.
Gladness flows into his heart.

MESSAGE TO PLANET ZEN...

What do I see on a summer's day...

Row, row the boat,
Slowly along slow flowing,
Shallow water.

On the banks of the
Stream wild plants
Are growing.
A breeze blows gently.

A toad croaks and jumps.
A little mouse
Scampers busily in the undergrowth.

"I like this. It is relaxing."

Read and write these 'oa' and 'ow' words.

road	load	loaded	loading	boat
boating	coat	coated	goat	moat
throat	cloak	croak	stoat	loan
Joan	moan	coal	shoal	float
approach	approached	coach		

snow	row	bow	low	crow
grow	growing	slowly	snowing	own
blow	blowing	flow	flowing	glow
glowing	show	showing	mellow	bellow
bellowing	shallow	fellow	hollow	follow
following	gallows	followed	following	throw
throwing	window			

Time for a test.

READ	COPY	COVER & SPELL
road		
load		
loaded		
coach		
boat		
boating		
coat		
croak		
goat		
moat		
throat		
cloak		
stoat		
loan		
Joan		
moan		
coal		
shoal		
float		
approach		

READ	COPY	COVER & SPELL
snow		
bow		
row		
low		
crow		
grow		
own		
slowly		
own		
blow		
flow		
glowing		
mellow		
show		
bellow		
shallow		
fellow		
hollow		
follow		
throwing		
window		

CHALLENGE EIGHTEEN

"Wow... that is an awesome dinosaur!"

Zoggy watches a movie. He goes back in time and meets a dinosaur with massive jaws to learn 'au' and 'aw' sounds.

Zoggy says,

"What can I do to teach you 'aw' and 'au' sounds?"

Let me mow the **lawn.**

Get up at **dawn.**

Sit and **draw.**

Drink with a **straw.**

Watch baby **crawl.**

Wear a pink **shawl.**

Go to sea in a **trawler.**

Train as a **lawyer.**

Visit a **haunted** house.

Launch a boat.

Drive an **automatic** car.

Walk in the **autumn** leaves -

To see a flying **saucer.**

MESSAGE TO PLANET ZEN...

I am watching a movie. In the film, an awesome dinosaur comes back to life and saunters along a street on planet earth. It yawns and shows an open jaw with a row of sharp, jagged teeth, making the audience scream. The naughty dinosaur film is based on a famous author's book.

Read and write these 'au' and 'aw' words.

August	awe	Paul	frog spawn	taught
naughty	strawberry	dinosaur	shawl	author
haughty	haul	awesome	crawl	autumn
awful	lawyer	caught	audio	paw
trawler	saunter	saw	yawn	audience
jaws				

Complete the list:

au	aw
dinosaur	jaws

CHALLENGE NINETEEN

Zoggy says " Ea is a mean, mean sound.
It is the master of disguise."

Zoggy says,

"ea can sound like the 'ea' in bread."

MESSAGE TO PLANET ZEN...

Fred eats bread, spread with chocolate spread, and makes a dreadful mess.

Heather, as light as a feather, hates this dreadful weather. She treads carefully because the path is treacherous.

Zoggy says,

"I told you 'ea' is really mean. Sometimes it sounds like 'ea' in dear..."

MESSAGE TO PLANET ZEN...

Oh dear me!

This earth kid, Beatrice, has lost her homework. It has clearly disappeared and it is nearly time to go to school. Tears! Fear!

"or the 'ea' in earth..."

Some earth kids rise up early to work to earn money. Then, they go to school to do more learning.

"or the 'ea' in break..."

An earth boy says, "When I break up for half term, it is great, because I can have breakfast late."

"or the 'ea' in bear."

Zoggy thinks that if he was not an alien, he would be a bear. He would not have to care what he would wear or if he had a tear in his shirt.

Read and write these 'ea' words.

bread	spread	dreadful	Heather
weather	tread	treacherous	feather

| earth | early | earn | learning |

dear	clear	Beatrice	disappeared
tears	fear	nearly	

| break | great | breakfast |

| bear | wear | tear |

Time for a test.

READ	COPY	COVER & SPELL
bread		
spread		
dreadful		
Heather		
feather		
weather		
tread		
treacherous		
earth		
early		
earn		
learning		
dear		
clear		
Beatrice		
disappeared		
nearly		
tears		
fear		
break		
great		
breakfast		
bear		
wear		
tear		

CHALLENGE TWENTY

On a fine day you can learn more about magic 'e'. It is a shame I can't swim in a lake.

MESSAGE TO PLANET ZEN...

On fine days, earth kids rake up pine cones that have fallen from the tree.

On fine days, earth kids compete outside. They write clues to make a treasure hunt.

On fine days, earth kids skate on their roller blades on the concrete in the park.

On fine days, when the sky is pure blue, earth people drive out to the theme park.

On fine days, earth people bake scones and cakes and eat them on paper plates.

Magic 'e' JUMPS BACK two letters and makes the vowel long.

a becomes A

e becomes E

i becomes I

o becomes O

u becomes U

e.g.   hat   becomes   hate

I hate hats.

Add magic 'e'.

pin	pine
pet	Pete
man	mane
fir	fire
tub	tube
hat	…………………
cub	…………………
mop	…………………
tap	…………………
rat	…………………
win	…………………
hop	…………………
cap	…………………

Make magic 'e' words...

Here are some initial sounds and blends.

b	c	f	l	m	r	s
t	sh	st	sp	sn	br	dr

...ace	...ade	...ate	...me	...ave	...ale
	made		same		
	fade		lame		

h	b	z	c	st	g	sc
t	dr					

...one	...ome	...oke	...ove	...ore	...ole

d	j	t	pr	f	c	l
fl	r	m	t	c		

...ube	...ule	...ute	...use	...une

b	p	t	h	sp	l	tr
m	str					

...ike	...ime	...ite	...use	...upe	...ide	...ine

CHALLENGE TWENTY ONE

Zoggy has a good view to teach you 'ue' and 'ew'.

Zoggy says,

"What can I do to teach you 'ew' and 'ue' sounds?"

I can sit in the **nature** reserve and use my **new** binoculars to **view** rare species of bird. He **viewed** it, as it **flew** by in the **blue** sky, and he watched it land and lick up drops of **dew** in its beak.

MESSAGE TO PLANET ZEN...

What a view

A few people enjoy chewing gum but they spit it out on the pavements.

Litter is strewn everywhere: last week, bits of old newspaper blew along the street.

It is true, there is a smell of glue from the factory up the road.

Queues of people wait for a long overdue bus, while the bus crew are drinking a brew in the cafe, but don't tell anyone I saw this.

Time for a test.

READ	COPY	COVER & SPELL
nature		
new		
view		
viewed		
flew		
blue		
dew		
chew		
chewing		
strewn		
few		
newspaper		
drew		
glue		
queues		
clue		
crew		
brew		

CHALLENGE TWENTY TWO

Zoggy says,

"c and g are the only two letters of the alphabet that can be hard and soft - <u>c</u>at and <u>d</u>og have hard sounds. The soft sound for 'c' is 's'. The soft sound for 'g' is 'j'. The sounds 'ce', 'ci', 'cy', 'ge', 'gi', and 'gy' are always soft - <u>mi</u>ce and <u>g</u>iant."

Zoggy says,

I think mice are nice.

Teaches you soft ce.

c sounds like s in ce, ci and cy.

George the ginger cat sits under the hedge.

Teaches you soft g.

g sounds like j in ge, gi and gy.

Other c and g words have a hard sound - 'cat' and 'got'.

Zoggy says,

"What can I do to teach you soft c *(like ce, ci, cy - s)* and soft g sounds *(ge, gi, gy - j)*?"

- Ride a bicycle
- Visit the city
- Eat ice cream
- Dance and prance
- Ride in a police car
- Ride in an ambulance
- Avoid all accidents

I want to:

- Work in a garage
- Visit the gym
- Eat sponge cake
- Live in a village
- Sit under a hedge
- Own a ginger cat called George
- Own a digital camera
- Embrace danger
- Be a gentleman

Zoggy spies a notice that reads, "COME TO THE FAIR."

What is happening on earth?

The police and an ambulance are there, the fire service are also there, but there is no danger - neither a fire or an accident. It is strange!

Earth kids are dressed up in fancy dress - as prince and princesses. Gina has won a prize.

Some ladies are selling sponge cake and groceries at reduced prices.

Zoggy decides to go on the bouncy castle, but he has no change. In fact, he has no money at all.

He needs the exercise, so he races on and starts to bounce, but he has not paid, so a policeman is coming over.

George the ginger cat sits under the hedge looking on and on...

Time for a test.

READ	COPY	COVER & SPELL
trace		
mice		
lace		
pace		
nice		
brace		
face		
Lucy		
receive		
perceive		
Nancy		
race		
huge		
fringe		
page		
gypsy		
huge		
rage		
beige		
danger		
stranger		
angel		
garage		
village		
cabbage		
postage		

Time for a test.

READ	COPY	COVER & SPELL
success		
December		
princess		
access		
Facebook		
necessary		

Zoggy says, "Let's look at all the sounds in my spelling toolbox."

He has some funny phonic sounds that include:

1. ar   or   ur   ir   er
2. ai as in rain   ay as in day
3. oi as in boil   oy as in boy
4. oo as in food   oo as in wood
5. oa as in coat   ow as in snow
6. ou as in mouse   ow as in owl
7. aw as in paw   au as in Uncle Paul
8. ee as in tree   ea as in treat

    ei as in receipt

9. ew as in few   ue as in true